POETIK PENETRATION
Passion - Pain - Possibilities

Amaris Bee

Eargasmic Ink Atlanta, Georgia

Copyright @ 2012 by Amaris Bee

All rights reserved. No part of this book may be reproduced or used in any form, electric or mechanical, including recording, photocopying, or by any information storage or retrieval system, without permission in writing from the author.

ISBN-13:
978-0615606262 (Eargasmic Ink)

ISBN-10:
0615606261

Cover and Interior Photography by Cherelle Scott
And D. Denise Peterson
Back Cover Photography by Andre Barrington
Models: Sakinah Colonel, Ellis Stanley, Cleveland Graham, Robin Grant, and Sirron Wood
Graphic Designer: Ayanna Card

First Edition
Printed in the United States of America
Eargasmic Ink
Atlanta, Georgia

Dedication

To All the Men I Never

Loved Before

And to the man that will one day

Be mine forevermore

Acknowledgements

I thank God for blessing me with the talent

I thank my dad for encouraging me
To always pursue my dreams

I thank my mom for my creativity
and writing skills

I thank my friends
for being on my praise team

And to everyone else
that has supported my cause
I appreciate you all

God Bless

To the Readers:

Several of these poems were inspired by gentlemen that have been a part of my life

Some poems were written right after my divorce when I was in an "Angry Black Woman" kind of mood

Others were written for friends or just because

If you are offended by profanity, nudity, or any sexual act please do not read any further, please close this book and step away…
if you are still reading then enjoy

CONTENTS

Passion

On a Heap of Dirty Clothes	13
The Netherlands	14
Love @ the Workjob	15
K.I.S.S.	16
Who am I?	18
Don't Ask Me	19
A Natural High	20
Midnite Talks	21
I'm Buzzing	22
Reminiscing	23
Kiss my Lips	24
Sugababycocopop	25
Thighs	26
The Threesome	27
Thoughts of You	28
Do Me	29
Under Construction	30
To Sir with Love	31
At First Glance	32
What is Foreplay?	33

Pain

Bustas	37
False Starter	38
Always on Your Mind	39
Low Tolerance for Bullshit	40
The Apology	41
Love is Not Enough	42
The Break Up Poem	44
I Never Loved You	46
Raped	47
A Letter to Reginald	48
U Doin to Much	50
To Marcus	51
Cut Off	52
What's the Problem?	53
One Night Stands	54
Size 22 Shoe	56
The Basketball Coach	58
To All the Menz	59
Rain	60
The Vow	61

Possibilities

Interpretations	65
How do I Know?	66
The Perfect Man 4 Me	67
No Questions Asked	68
Being in Love	69
Hey You	70
Stay (Her)	71
Stay (Him)	72
Friday Nite Lites	73
Be Mine	74
You are Love	75
The Slender of a Man	76
Alphabet Love	77
The Prenup	78
Come Holla at Me	80
Good Morning Sunshine	82
Bi Polar Love	84
Quit Her	86
Eight Minutes of Bondage	87
Addickted	88
The Possibilities of Love	89

POETIK PENETRATION

Passion - Pain - Possibilities

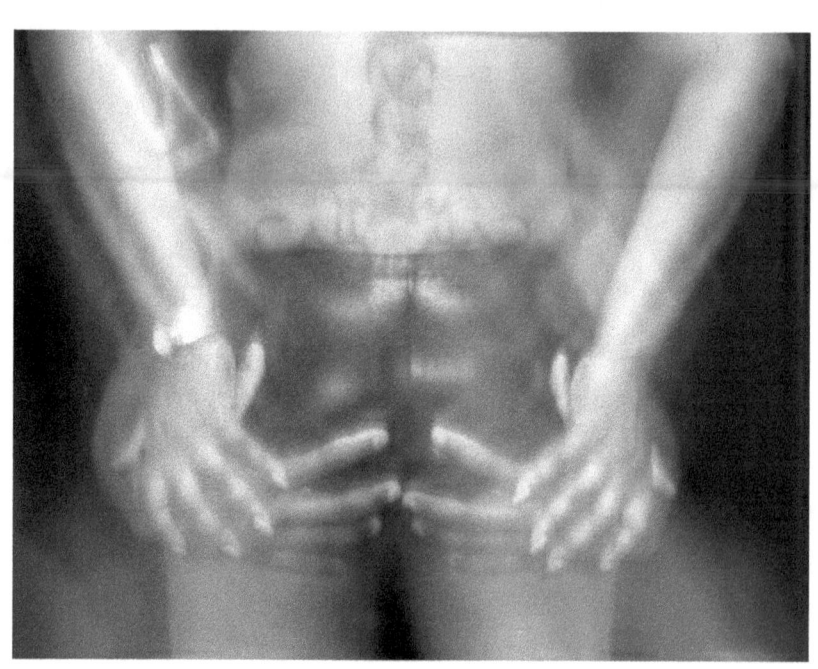

PASSION

On a Heap of Dirty Clothes

You are the coals in my grill
And I miss the thrill
Of you igniting the fire in my soul

Remember the first time
you asked me to dance
And the next thing I knew
you had snatched off my pants
I never dreamed my first time
would precede romance

But there was none and that was OK
Cause as time went by you were just a lay

You were never my boyfriend…
I was never your girl
Never went on a date
but you still rocked my world

And to this day three years have passed
You got a lady and I got a man
But you still keep beggin' for this ass

Aint it a shame we both were too lame
To realize that we were in love
With each other…my brother
Didn't hit us 'til it was too late

So what should we do? I guess like Badu
I'll see U next lifetime and when I do
I won't resist the love I feel still exists.

The NETHERLANDS

I met this guy the other day
With these big brown eyes
He had dimples and a smile
That would warm the coldest heart

His hair…angora
His features…keen
He came from Africa, India
The NETHERLANDS, somewhere who knows?
His chest, his back, his bow legs, his hands
Strong, dark, and lovely

He spoke and he made me laugh
He winked and made me blush
He hugged me and his scent drove me crazy
He kissed me and my heart started to race
He undressed me and I him
He stared at me and I stared at him
Both amazed
He lay on top of me and I started to sweat
He licked my lips I tasted his tongue
Lobes were nibbled and nipples licked
He touched my inner passion and brought me to tears
The best of the best
Wish it could have lasted
For years
The NETHERLANDS
The only place to be…

Love @ the Workjob

Is this you in my grill each day?
Stopping by my office just to say, "Hey!"
Looking so fine in your three piece suit
Making sure I know that U look cute?

Is this you going out of your way
To lift my spirits when I feel gray
Giving me pep talks whenever I'm down
When I feel like quitting and leaving town?

Running your fingers through my hair
Constantly showing me that you care
Staring at me with those big brown eyes
Making me laugh 'til I hurt my sides

Is this you always tempting me?
Pushing the limits to the nth degree
As we converse about various things
Sometimes I regret we both wear rings

K.I.S.S.

Daddy's mustache would scratch my face
Mommy's were short, quick pecks on the cheek
Grandma's were wet and sloppy…eek!?

One on the hand by my admirers
First one on the lips was quick and dry
But they improved as time went by

Soft lips, chapped lips, candy taste, stank breath
Braces, straight perfect pearly whites
Have you been chewing on rocks?
Or were you just in a fight?

Not enough lip-Too much tongue
Oh wait that's just right baby
Come here and give me some

On the back of my neck
On the front of my chest
One on each of my beautiful breasts

One down there
Are we movin too fast?
Just don't bite it or I'll kick yo black ass

Bruise my lips, floss my teeth
Thrust your tongue
Up in me

Lick the black off my back
Make me scream until I lose my voice
Make me love you so I'll have no choice

But to love you back
Suck and withdraw the life out of me
Deposit love and honesty

Your kiss makes me hollow as a shell
Fill me up like I was before I fell
For your deathly, passionate, kiss

Keep it Soft and Sensual

Who am I?

I am that ho on the pole
I'm why your wallet has a hole
Where your money used to be
Now all your paycheck comes to me
Oh if your wife only knew
Bout all the freaky shit we do
She'd probably cuss, scream and shout
And finally put your dumb ass out

I am that bitch at the club
The one on stage up at the pub
I shake my ass everyday
Because my day job just don't pay
Gimme $10 for a tabletop
I'll freak you down till you say, "Stop"
Just remember that you can't touch
Or Joe the bouncer will fuck you up

I am that classic prostitute
And that's my pimp in the leisure suit
Waiting for me to make a sale
So he can get Quanda outta jail
It'll be 60 for a blow
225 for a whole dam show
Or if you just want to fuck
Then that will be 100 bucks

But even though I am a ho
I'm someone's daughter and although
I shake my ass at the club
I got three kids and a hub
And inasmuch as I sell my ass
I was Valedictorian of my class
If women got paid like the men
We wouldn't be in this predicament

Don't Ask Me

Pay close attention as I squat
To give a lil lesson about my twat
If you look real close you'll see a dot
Yeah dat right dere dat's the spot
It's called a clit
It should be licked
Gently stroked b4 you stick
In the dick
If you come too quick
I guarantee that I'll be sick

Now on to lesson two
Of my anatomy and what to do
To ensure that I am pleased
To have me beggin on my knees
There's another zone that's called the G spot
And when you hit it- it will get hot
If I shudder & twitch it's all good …if not
It means I haven't come yet and you've got
To start all over so please do not
Ask me if I came yet cuz you might get shot

a natural high

do u ever wonder what it's like
what it's like to be in me
to be in me and on me
up in me upon me
within me without me
out and throughout me
up under me over me
above and all over me
by me beside me
to sex me and ride me?

ever ponder or wonder
what we could be or would be
cuz i think of you every day
all the time, constantly
you begin and you end me
when you love me you send me
your passion ascends me
on a natural high

Midnite Talks

My pussys drippin wet from you
Fillin my head with thoughts of you
Doing thangs to my body
you aint got no business doin

You have got my head fucked up
It starts each nite with a "Hey"- "Wuzzup?"
Next thing I know, I am dreamin
of us straight up in the buck

I can't even concentrate
On the shit I need to do
Every time I meditate
my thoughts end up rite back on you

What is going on with me?
I just cannot understand
How can I be caught up
by the conversation of a man

We aint even did shit yet
Hell our lips aint even met
You got me like Pavlov's dogs
the phone rings and my pussy's wet

Again…again…again…again…again

I'm Buzzing

Stop!... Don't touch me
Let me just lay here in the wet spot
I'm trying to recover my Lover

No... quit playin!
Let me just bask in the afterglow of you
No words to say, just let me lay

Let me get my breath back
Cause I sound like I just ran a marathon
But I had so much fun

The smell of boodussy is in the air
I look like Don King by the hair
And I don't even really care
All I know is I don't want to share

Your dick... with nobody else
Cause what you got is addicktive
Your lovin's like PCP, Like crack to me

And I'm fuckdrunk- Buzzing off your dick
I'm High as a kite in the sky
On a windy day
and it's OK

All I want is you
In between my thighs
Like a slip and slide
Can we go on another ride?

Cause I don' wanna lose this high

Reminiscing

I know it's been years
It's been a long time
But every blue moon
You do cross my mind

I remember the good times
The moments we shared
The way that you laughed
And how much you cared

About me and my family
And all of my friends
I miss you so much
Wish we could begin

From the first day we met
All over again
I often times wonder
Where you have been?

Where did you go
When you left my life?
Do you have kids now
A house, car, and wife?

Or are you alone too
Writing def poetry
Sitting 'round wondering
What happened to me?

Kiss my Lips

My mind is wandering to thoughts of you
Kissing my neck and licking my ear
My thoughts drift off to wishing you
Would run your fingers through my hair

And pull my head back to kiss my lips

I am yearning to feel you smell your scent
Inhale your breath til I'm content
I'm waiting for you to part my thighs
To draw me closer as I close my eyes

And push my hair back to kiss my lips

I'm craving for you to enter me
When we are one you center me
I want to feel you come into me
Grab me like I was meant for thee

And yank my head back to kiss my lips

Sugababy Cocopop

You're my sugababy cocopop

Sweet potato pumpkin pie

Chocolate honey bunch of oats

Candy apple of my eye

Marshmallow cup cake

Caramel boo

Sweet baby sweet baby

I love you

Thighs

Look between my thighs
You'll find a big fat clit
Waiting on u
to give it a lick
Waiting on your thick
big juicy ass black dick
To stick it in my slit
and I want to cum quick
Oh my goodness
it's a perfect fit
Beat da pussy up
til I tell yo ass to quit
Oh baby baby
u is da shit
But shawty so am I
And don't chu forget it

The Threesome

After watching years of sex tapes
I've always had this fantasy
Of having two fine ass guys
Freak me down straight ecstasy

I want them to be hetero
and only cater to and pamper me
I have the perfect pair of guys
To make this dream a reality

One is a friend of a friend
Who texts me pictures of his pecs
The other one is an ol classmate
Who always likes to flex

They best of friends like brothers
Oh and if they only knew
They could of fucked me the other day
When they was at my house drankin brew

They can do me any which way they want
All night long and then all day
They can fuck me til I can't take no more
I mean what more can I say

It may never happen but if it does
I will let you know and that's no lie
Cause that's something on my bucket list
To do you both before I die

Thoughts of You

I am lying in water
White foam atop
Hot to relax me
With moscato in my left hand
And a pen in my right
I write this poem to you

Starting to drift off
I dream of places
Never seen before
Wanting to forget the reality
Of my everyday world
I close my eyes and think of you

As the jets hit my back
And massage away my worries
I wonder how I can get away
From all life's drama and mess
Then I think of how you love me
And a smile graces my face

Do Me

Spank me
Grab me
Slap me
Hold me

Bang me
Cuff me
Fuck me
Choke me

Pull my hair
Smack my ass
Smoke me out
Like a blade of grass

Stick me
Lick me
Fool me
Trick me

Prick me
Dick me
Freak me
Pick me

Sexing you
Is not a sin
Do me baby
One mo' gin

Under Construction

Hello is this the construction man?
How soon can you get here?
I really need you to come over
I've got some things in need of repair

What's wrong? Oh I have a list of things
That I need for you to check
My heat don't burn my pipes are clogged
And I need some wood on my deck

As soon as you walk through the door
I want your tool in your hand
I need you to fix me up
Cuz I'm broken "Mr. Fix It" man

I want you to hammer me
Then drill me
Nail me to the wall
And thrill me

Make sure you're wearing your hard hat
It's always safety first
You've got the blueprints to my body
Hurry up cuz I'm bout to burst

I need you to do some screwing
Bring some pliers to open me wide
Jackhammer these walls boy
Till you've busted it up inside

To Sir with Love

He grabbed me by my hips
And pulled me towards his lips
The sheets I had to grip
As he teased me with the tip

Of his tongue then came the drip
Drip drop wetness skinny-dipped
My nectar he then sipped
His nature he then slipped

Into me and then he flipped
Me over
well equipped
By no means was I gypped
I think I may be whipped

At First Glance

The very first second I saw your face
I lost all concepts of time and space
It was a strange unfamiliar place
Time seemed to slow down to a turtle's pace

I don't think there will ever be
Any man that compares to thee
Love at first glance you're my destiny
You are everything to me

Your smile it beams and brightens my day
No words can express what I want to say
I need you here; need your company
You make me whole in every way

What is Foreplay?

Hands n hair
and hands down there
Kisses on lips
and kisses on hips
Your scent
Your taste
Your gaze
Your stare
Us hunching
in our underwear

Pain

Bustas

I'm sorry but I just don't seem to recall
You fuckin me...maybe your dick was so small
That I didn't know that you were in me at all
I'm trying to remember but I just can't recall

You lied to my boyfriend and then told my girl
"I beat her down good...I rocked that hoe's world"
I heard I sucked your dick and made your toes curl
Heard it was so dam good that my head start to swirl

Somebody told me I had on handcuffs
A whip and a chain cause I like it rough
You know what playa I've heard quite enough
I am tired of you telling these lies on my 'stuff'

What really went down on that hot summer day
Was U on me...that was nice I must say
I hugged you, you kissed me, we rolled in the hay
You came twice in your boxers while we were at play

But let it be known that we did NOT screw
Nor was I chained up like a beast in a zoo
The whole existence of my time spent with you
Was so unforgettable...what's your name again Boo?

False Starter

I started to…

Call you last night
Cook you some dinner
Take you to Tampa
Say you look thinner

Buy you a bracelet
Sing you a song
Write you a poem
Bout how I'm wrong

I started to…

Come by to see you
Ask you to dances
Get you a Mai Tai
Help your finances

Apologize
For my excuses
But I cannot cause
I am straight clueless

Always on Your Mind

Have you ever met someone
Who aint got nuthin to do
But sit and gossip
And worry bout you?

I mean how insecure, jealous
And trifling can you be
To waste time everyday
Sittin round talking bout me

Why are you so concerned
About who I'm wit
What I'm doing, where I am going
When I go take a shit?

Bitch please!...
Not only do I not give a dam about you
I could care less what you say
And gives a dam what you do

If my name and bizness
Is in your mouth all the time
Then hell- I feel a bit flattered
That I'm always on your mind

Low Tolerance for Bullshit

I will not be disrespected
I will not be called out my name
I possess too much dam confidence
To let you cause me pain

I will not allow you to make me feel
As if I am inferior
Because your sorry, trifling ass
Thinks that you are superior

I will not tolerate a man who lies
I can't have a spouse who cheats
Cause a negro who can't keep his dick in his pants
Won't survive being married to me

I'm a strong Black woman with a house and a car
I got four dam college degrees
Besides fixing things and sexing me
What da fuck can u do for me?

I have a low tolerance for bullshit
I'm too good to put up with your mess
So if you step to me you besta bring it
Cause I refuse to accept anything less

And if my expectations are too high 4 u
Then that means ur not "the one"
I would rather be all by myself
Than to "settle" for just anyone

The Apology

I'm tired of buying shades
For a black and blue eye
I'm sick of people constantly
Asking me why
I stay with you…
Why I put up with your cheating
Your drinking, your smoking
And your 10 PM beatings
I don't wanna hear
No more got dam excuses
Don't want no rationale
For all your abuses
You don't have to say you're sorry
No dam more
I been known your ass was sorry
So you can keep your
Apology

Love is Not Enough

You can love somebody with all your heart
You can love a man with all of your soul and mind
You can give your all to make a relationship work
You can give all your money and all of your time

But love won't pay the bills won't stop him from cheating
Won't stop him from stealing won't stop him from beating
Won't stop him from loving Yolanda, Tina and Kim
Won't make him love you the way that you love him

Love cannot change a man whose been doing the same ol thing for years & years
Don't lie to yourself, don't be in denial, you got to see the bullshit through your tears
I pray to God that He will reveal the truth to you…open up your ears so you can hear
What I'm trying to tell you my sister is lose the fear
Love is NOT enough my dear

I said Love is not enough, is not enough, is not enough
If you don't wake up you're gonna lose all your stuff
(your job, your house, your car)
Enough is enough!!!!
Sometimes you gotta let go of a nightmare in order to reach your dreams
Sometimes you gotta be BY yourself to learn to love yourself or so it seems

Stop lying to yourself because you're trying to convince yourself to stay with a toxic man
Stop lying to me cause I know the truth
Let the truth set you free so that you can stand

On your own two feet ...

the break up poem

If we broke up a YEAR ago
Then why are u still calling my phone?
There was a reason why I left yo ass
So hang up the phone and leave me ALONE

Why the HELL are you still calling me?
I don't want to BE with you.
I thought I made that clear
when I was leaving you
What will it take for me
to get that through to you?
That we are done, that we are through

Motherfucker u got one mo time
To call my house, to call my job, to call my cell
Am I gonna have to call the cops
So they can come and put your ass in jail?
What the HELL is goin on?
I'm in denial that ur in denial
That we is over over over over

Dear Lord I pray EVERYDAY
That He will send a pretty girl your way
So U can forget about me
forget about WE
forget I exist
So you won't resist
the fact that WE no longer exist
Stop trying to persist
Cuz U beginning to act a little stalkerish

So let me take this time to SPELL it out
Cause you can't hear the words that's coming out my mouth
You can't take a hint
You aint get the memo
You didn't get the message
You don't have a clue

I- B- R- O- K- E- U- P- W- I- T- H- Y – O - U

I Never Loved You

I never loved you
Even though I told you so
After seven years together
I just thought I'd let you know

I never loved you
I don't know why U think I would
You're a cheater and a liar
You just aint a bit of good

Maybe that's why when you left me
I never shed a tear
Unconsciously I was relieved
Ur dumb ass wasn't here

I never loved you
Took me a while to realize
That what we had was nothing
A waste of time—of yours and mines

I wish I'd never met you
Made your acquaintance or saw your face
I wish I could forget that you
Exist and take up space

I never loved you
I tried but then I quit
When I snapped back to reality
And remembered that you aint shit

I never loved you
Even though I told you so
I'm so glad that you are gone
And I just thought I'd let you know

raped

he raped me with his look

the way he stared, his eyes

if looks could talk then they would say

"I vant to lick your thighs"

I felt so violated

I start to run and hide

what were you really thinking

when you saw me walking by?

A Letter to Reginald

I was in love with you
And then from outer space
Some long lost foreign place
Out came the truth

That you were not alone
Belonged to someone else
You flat out lied to me
Lied to my face

My heart was crushed in two
Straight ripped up out my chest
I was so dam depressed
Thought you were mine

So I had to let you go
Even though I loved you so
Didn't have the strength to fight
Not at the time

Then I received the news
Thought you were finally free
I heard you left your wife
Thought I had a chance

My heart was overjoyed
My love would come to me
Soul mate I'd thought you be
Perfect romance

So I gave you some time
Time to enjoy yourself
Waited for your text, email
Call on the phone

Guess what it never came
And then I got the news
You married someone else
I'm still alone

What happened to the love
I thought you had for me
Look me straight in the eye
Was it all a lie?

I was in love with you
I guess it wasn't true
Just wanted you to know
You broke my heart in two

U Doin Too Much

Ever been lying in bed?
Headboard is banging ya head
You looking up at the ceiling
And then to yourself you said
This fool is doing too much
Tryin to be over the top
He spending way too much energy
I'm bout to ask him to stop.

You ever been in the act?
Your boyfriends choking you out
You feel like you finta die
Feel like you just fought a bout
When is the bell gonna ring?
I'm waiting to hear that "DING"
This round's officially over
Fat lady is bout to sing

Am I gon have to go out
And hire a dam referee
To call out all of your fouls
And all your sex penalties?
You make when u fuckin me
Time out…hell flag on the play
You gotsta go you can't stay
I mean what more can I say?

To Marcus

It wasn't your fault that I fucked you
I fucked you on my own free will
It wasn't your fault that the condom broke
But it IS your fault that I was ill

Over the years I have forgiven you
For all the pain that you have caused
But I'm still pissed off at your sorry ass
Cuz you're a cowardly bitch with no balls

All you had to do was tell me
That you had a dirty ass dick
At least I would of had the choice to decide
Whether or not I wanted to get sick

I shoulda sued your ass for doctor's fees
For the cost of meds I had to take
For stealing a piece of my confidence
And for a friendship that was obviously fake

Every time I see your face
I wanna bust yo ass in the mouth
And every time you see me out
You run like a scared little mouse

You can't even look me in my face
Cause you don't have the nerve
But u best believe mutha fucka
You gon get exactly what u deserve

Cut Off

At the party, just walked in
I go up to the bar and I see an old friend
I walk up to him with a smile on my face
He looks at me like I'm from a distant place

"I'm here with somebody"
I said, "Huh, come again?"
He shouts, "I'm here with somebody"
So I back up and extend my hand

"Oh well it's good to see you"
I awkwardly say
I get my drink from the bar
And begin to sashay

My way cross the room
To where my girls all sit
And I'm thinking
"WTF? Was that all about…shit"

Did you think I was going to jump u
Or hunch your leg like Rover?
I can't hug you in public?
Just last week u bent me over

I could care less that you are here
With somebody else-u r so cat
I know how to stay in my lane
You aint got to front like that

That was SO dam rude of you
You need to learn some tact
You know what u just got cut off
Yup it's as simple as that

What's the Problem?

Are my toes not cute?
Does my breath stank?
Do I snore too loud?
Is my pussy rank?

Am I too dam chunky?
Or am I way too fat?
Are my legs too hairy?
U don't like dis cat?

I'm trying to figure out
Why u won't kiss me
You won't eat me out
U just not into me?

Are u not feeling this?
Am I just not your type?
Do you like lil boys?
Am I not what u like?

U tryin to take it slow?
Why did you push pause?
Is there somebody else?
Tryin to get in they draws?

U just want friendship?
I got enough friends
I'm bout to chuck the deuces
Can't make u want dis end

One Night Stands

This is a story bout one night stands
Some were very good and some were very bad

The first one was during my college years
Fell asleep with my thighs stuck to his ears
But when I woke up he was all up in me
Couldn't feel a thing went back to sleepin

The 2nd dude I met at the Lounge of Leopard
He had on a hoodie he looked like a shepherd
We went to my house and before u know
It was WWF and I was in the figure four

Went to #3's house to get some crab legs
Next thing u know I was standin on my head
The crazy part is when we were done
He took me upstairs to meet his son

The 4th was my girlfriend's next door neighbor
Tall dark and handsome sumthin to savor
He tried to get my goods but I kept sayin no
He had a wifey and a baby so it was a no go

The 5th little dude was a chemistry major
One parent Black the other from Asia
Had long pretty hair like Polamalu
Smelled like peaches and apple shampoo

I can't even recall #6's name
I guess cause the sex was oh so lame
All I can remember is he worked at a gym
He had a fine ass body but his dick was slim

I met #7 at a party with some strippers
He hugged me round the neck and started playin with my zipper
He was just 25 a young whipper snapper
I felt like a video ho with a rapper

Number 8 was a dear old friend
I met him in college when I wasn't giving in
Saw him online and thought we'd reconnect
We had unfinished business…overdue sex

The ninth one's name was a luxury car
After we did it he said I lived too far
I drove to his house and I agreed
So that was the last time we did the deed

Number 10's house was oh so stank
Trash on the floor and dishes in the sink
He couldn't get it up and I was so glad
I almost threw up cuz the smell was so bad

A little advice to all of my girlfriends
Don't have sex unless u know him
Sometimes it just aint worth the hassle
U may get a prince or a royal asshole

Size 22 Shoe

We had excellent conversations
Spent hours on the telephone
I was attracted by his intelligence
In his 20's yet he was full grown

When I first met this tall strapping man
I couldn't help but look at his feet
He wore a size 22 shoe
So I knew I was in for a treat

After months and months of dating
And flirting over the phone
I finally went to visit him
And he welcomed me into his home

He rubbed my shoulders and my back
Like he worked at Spa Sowell
We drank 2 glasses of Shiraz
And by then I was horny as hell

He kissed my neck and then my lips
Next thing I know I was outta my clothes
He escorted me to his bedroom
The deal was about to be closed

Or so I thought until I saw his dick
Shocked and devastated was I
I needed a magnifying glass
I felt like I was bout to die

I thought to myself don't panic
Maybe with some help it will grow
But even after it was hard as a rock
It was tiny and thin and just gross

So I tried to play it off
All of a sudden I became sick
A message to all who read this
Big feet does not equal big dick

The Basketball Coach

My girlfriend called me one sunny day
"Got a guy that I want you to meet."
If I had of known they used to kick it
I would have never agreed to see the creep

Now looking back I oft wonder why
She thought that I would like him at all
We didn't have a dam thing in common
We were so incompatible

He had a fucked up bitch ass attitude
and was constantly bringing me down
We argued just about everything
And he always wore a frown

The most negative man that I've ever met
I broke it off without saying a word
I really didn't have that much to say
He got on my got dam nerves

To All the Menz

To all the men I never loved before
Y'all aint nothing but a bunch of whores
Y'all ninjas make me sick
Always thinking with your dick
This is for all the men who tried to score

To all u bruhs that came up in my house
Who lied and told me u aint have no spouse
I feel sorry for your wives
And ya fucked up trifling lives
Y u even walking through my door?

To all u ninjas cheesin in my face
To those that breathe and take up space
You are such a waste of time
What the fuck was on my mind?
You would think I had more class and taste

To all you sorry punk ass bunch of menz
Who I can't rely, trust on, or depend
Until you do right by me
Your dreams they will never be
I raise this glass, propose a toast to thee

Cheers Bitchez….

Rain

Rain, rain, rain
Splash upon my window pane
Wash away my fears
Wash away the tears
From my eyes

Rain, sweet, rain
Falling from a cloudy sky
Cold and windy gray
Reminds me of the day
I met you

I am so lonely
since you went away
All it has done
Since you left me is rain

Can I get some sunshine
To brighten my day ?
Please stop the pain
Stop the rain Stop the rain

The Vow

Do you take this man- This human, this being,
this imperfect person to be your mate?
Do you promise to be his loving new wife,
for the rest of your life, forever always?

Do you from this day…day forward commit,
to put up with shit…until your death date?
For better or worse, when worse is a curse
Take this here man for the rest of your days?

For richer or poorer…when there is no work,
bankruptcy, foreclosures, we can't make the rent
No job to be found, how long should it be,
before I say peace… when all money's spent?

In sickness and in health, with or without insurance,
whether you're ok or feeling blue
On this day I promise to love and to cherish,
my soul mate, my lover, my husband, I DO

Possibilities

interpretations

Do you see what I see
when u sit and stare at me?
Tell me what it is I hear
when u whisper in my ear?

When we lie in bed at night
I inhale your breath
U exhale mine right?

Bone of my bone - Flesh of my flesh
My old is your new your stale is my fresh

And so clean is our dream
Don't you know what I mean?

When I am in u and you are on me
Tell me can I feel your soul's energy

That inner chi that's in your genes
My synergy that's in your jeans

When I kiss u and u kiss me
Can you taste your uncertainty?

Interpret for me what it is I need
What it is u want-is it to be freed?

From limitations
Hesitations
Reservations
Stipulations
Interpretations

How do I know ?

How do I know I'm not Over U Yet?
When U came in the room my panties got wet

How do I know I'm not Over U Yet?
When U walked towards me I started to sweat

U gave me a hug- I don't want to let go
If U asked me to fuck U I couldn't say NO

Every time I look up
and my eyes see your face
My heart starts to pound-
my blood starts to race

When U sit next to me my legs start to shake
My hands start to tremble…my belly to ache

How do I know I'm not Over U Yet?
If U were for sale I'd go into debt

How do I know I'm not Over U Yet?
'Cause I feel the same way as the first day we met

The Perfect Man 4 Me

D'Angelo's bedroom eyes
Blair's smile and Tyson's thighs
Antonio's sex appeal
Keith's style and Prince's wheels

A set of Ginuwine's abs
Jamie's gift to gab
Barry's voice and L.L.'s lips
Tai's black back…his ass and hips

Denzel's personality
Silk's sensuality
Lorenzo's perfect skin of honey
All of Jordan's hard earned money

Marley's dreaded locks of hair
Omar's sexy haunting stare
Cosby's wisdom, Sisqo's moves
Stevie's talent and Wesley's groove

Shamar's pair of dimpled cheeks
Hathaway's mello smooth mystique
A heart of gold…a righteous soul
Commitment, pride, and valid goals

These are ingredients to my recipe
And just what would this creation be?

He'd be the PERFECT man 4 me

No Questions Asked

Ask me no questions I'll tell U no lies

I love you baby your soul & your mind

But most of all I love your heart

I wish that we would never part

I love your smile - I love your ways

The silly little things U do to make my days

Full of laughter

Full of life

Full of love

Being in Love

As snowflakes fall
From a seamless sky
I gaze out my window
Wondering why
Being in love is so complicated and perplexed

I remember the good times
We've had in the past
And constantly ponder how
Long will we last
Being in love is so convoluted and complex

How can a small word
Have a meaning so great
The power to destroy
And the ability to create
Being in love is so confusing and intricate

Hey You

My Boo
1 + 1 is 2
U don't have a clue
That I'm addicted to

Your smile, your eyes,
Your sexy chocolate thighs,
Your kiss, your size
You're not like other guys

Hey You-Woo woo

Oh if you only knew
I'm stuck to you like glue
I don't know what I'd do

Without your care
The moments that we share
I think you're unaware
That I wish you'd take me there

Stay (Her)

It's in her eyes

The window to her soul

The brightness of her smile

The bounce up in her stroll

It's all about the way

She moves its bout her sway

The silly things she say

That makes him want to stay

Stay (Him)

It's in his eyes

That sexy haunting stare

The sweet things that he do

To show her that he care

It's all about the way

He'll love her til she gray

The joy he gives each day

That makes her want to stay

Friday Nite Lites

It's Friday night

I'm all alone

Wishing you'd call me

On the phone

It's raining outside

I'm feeling depressed

I need U to come

Relieve my stress

I want to cry but

The tears won't come

I'm tired of being

in a slump

I'm too dam old

To play this game

This whole dating thing

Is oh so lame

Be Mine

Could you help a sista out? I'm in a bind

I don't have NO Valentine

Send me some flowers and a bottle of wine
Tell me I'm cute or tell me I'm fine
Sing me a song or write me a rhyme
Let's go out and have a good time!
Open my door… "Oh, you're so kind!"
A candlelight dinner on the pier at Nine
At midnight we're dancing down the Soul Train line
The next thing you know we can see the sunshine
Our date won't end with a bump and a grind
Just a simple hug and kiss would blow my mind
Lovin me to death is not a crime
You know a good catch is hard to find
Do U wish I was yours like I wish U was mine?
Won't you be my Valentine?

You are Love

I'd give you my last breath
I'd give you my last dime
I'd give you my very
Last second in time

I love you that much
With all of my heart
With all of my soul
With all of my mind

You are the water
That quenches my thirst
The fire within me
That energy burst

You're that soft cool breeze
On a hot summer day
You are Peace-You are Love
You're the Last - You're the First

the Slender of a Man

I love the slender of a man
The slender of his waist
The sway he walks- the way he talks
The splendor of his taste

I love the creases of a man
The creases tween his pecs
His chiseled back-that dam six pack
The pieces of his sex

I love his lips, his eyes, his ears, his thighs
His pinky finger and his pinky toe
His teeth, his tongue, his legs, his buns
I even love his hype ass fro

I love his smile
I love his style
I love it when he's silly
And I love it when he's wild

I love the essence of a man
The essence of his heart
The way he loves- we fit like gloves
The lessons he imparts

Alphabet Love

A is for All you say
your loving words I hear each day and
B your Baby face
That beaming smile lights up the place
C is for the Courage that I had
when I met you
D is for the Doubt I felt
when I aint think you loved me baby

EFGHI will always love you baby
JKLMNy one could of had you but you chose me
OPQR you gonna be there for me always?
STUVW just outta or XY I'll go cray Z

I will always be there through fair or foul weather
Alpha beta not break my heart
I can't stand it when we're apart
Alpha beta not leave me
Alpha beta not go away
Alpha beta not leave me or I'll die

the prenup

from head to toe if I was paralyzed
if I lost the vision that is in my eyes
could never hear U whisper in my ear
my arms my legs were just to disappear

If I wasn't able to have no kids
and if I could they would die of SIDS
if I lost all my money in the market crash
got accused of selling coke and smoking hash

lost my job, lost my car and my house
would U still be willing to be my spouse?
would U donate a kidney just to save my life?
that's all it takes for me to be your wife

I gotta know that you'll be there for me
if I lost all my hair and all of my teeth
them vows they say for better or worse
even if the worst seems like curse

if I started to stutter like Forest Gump
if the doctor said that he found a lump
if I wanted to go back to school
I need to know if you would love me fool

if I became abusive to myself
would U leave me alone or stay to help
I don't want no gotdam diamond ring
if U think that marriage is an easy thing

Don't even bother to get down on your knee
if U can't take a little pain & misery
marriage is more than love and happiness
sometimes it feels like a hot ass mess

U gotsta be willing to stick by my side
Thru troubled water U gotta be my guide
my light, my knight in shining armor
When I'm stressed out U gotsta be mo calmer

I need you to always protect me
And I want you to love me unconditionally
So if you can live up to this agreement without fear
Here's a pen and paper just sign right here

Come Holla at Me

When I walked into the room this evening …
I looked around and saw your face
I couldn't help but notice your smile
and right then I knew I wanted to place
On your juicy luscious lips
a sweet and tender kiss
I began to think about us
maybe hooking up a little later after this

Then you looked up and noticed me
I tried to act like I didn't see you on the sly
But I could feel your eyes undressing me
and I giggled to myself… oh my
I wondered if you were looking at my booty
or if you were mesmerized by my doo
I wanted to know what you were thinking-
if you want me like I want you

As I walked towards you I'm hoping
there's no ring on your left hand
Or a fresh tan line where it should be-
you know what I mean- you understand?
Cause the last thing I need is to be out with you
and end up on an episode of "Cheaters"
I mean look at me I'm 5 ft. tall if your wife starts a fight
I might not be able to beat her

I'm from the old school though when it comes to men
I refuse to make the first move
I want you to be sure that I'm what you want
so the chasing is for you to do

So as I get closer to you I flash a wink
and a brite smile your way
Basically that means (Hey I'm available.
I'm feeling you. Let's go get laid)

No I'm just playing-no I'm not- no but for real,
we don't have to have sex tonite
But I do think that would be an activity
we could enjoy together eventually alright?

Don't be nervous man I promise I won't bite –
unless you ask me to
So when I sit down from reading this here poem
you know what you need to do

Come holla at me

Good morning sunshine
Good morning sunshine

Even though I don't see you
I know ur safely nestled bove the clouds
in the sky

Even though its 10 degrees outside
I still feel your warmth upon my face
And I don't know why

Its morning sunshine
Morning sunshine

You've been there forever
As long as I can remember uve kissed me
Everyday

Sometimes u shine so brightly
I can not even look at you
Unless I wear shades

Morning sunshine
Good morning sunshine

In the evening when it's dark and cold
U r still there in my heart and soul
Another day goes by

And no matter what thru rain or hail
High winds and thunderstorms
U still r there for I

Still shining and caressing me
Still loving and blessing me

Making me hot making me sweat
Making things sticky making me wet

I need a fan turn up the AC
My temperature's rising shine your light on me

Good morning sunshine
Good morning sunshine

Good day!

Bi Polar Love

I'm discombobulated

This thing between us..it is north and south and east and west
It's up and down and right and left; it's just a hot ass mess
I say the sky is blue; you say its kinda bluish gray
I say hello; you say goodbye dear have a happy day

This shit is complicated

I don't know who you are from week to week; from day to day
You say you're leaving but you still here guess you're gonna stay
We fought the other day cause you was mad I left the house
But you're the one that told me to have fun and go hang out

I get intoxicated

By your smooth talking, sexy walking, soft ass kiss
You sex me down you put it on me and I take a risk
Every time the phone rings and I decide to take your call
I don't know why I put up with your crazy ass at all

Guess I've assimilated

Or just adjusted to the crazy shit you do each day
Does that make me insane for putting up with all your crazy ways?
I think of leaving you each day I wake up out my bed
But I'm scared to leave though 'cause you said you'd make me dead

Quit Her

Why don't you drop your girlfriend?
And try to talk to mine
I can guarantee you'll have a
Much much better time

I don't claim to be a psychic
Or a modern day cupid
But if you keep that current chick
Then you're just downright stupid

She treats you bad, always got drama
Every day and night
Just quit the bitch and leave
And date my friend alright?

Eight Minutes of Bondage

One	I am sitting in darkness
Two	with jazz in my ears
Three	I am bound I am frozen
Four	minutes seem like years
Five	Mmmm I can smell you
Six	I can also feel you near
Seven	untie me unleash me
Eight	release me from my fear

Addickted

Puff puff passin' pussy like weed
Takes one hit to get high indeed
High like Legend sittin' on cloud nine
Open her legs while I open your mind
You can get addickted to that dyme
Just like you do when u read my rhymes
Let me verbally fuck your mind
I'll give u eargasms every time

Come cum come cum come on
I got something to say that just might turn u on

A pilsner of brewsky; a glass of wine
A cup of my nectar honey divine
You can't stop drinking cuz it tastes so good
Like u can't put this book down understood
Lyrics bout men who treated me
Like shit and then straight up left the scene
Verses bout what love could possibly be
For all my sistas, my girls, and me

In out in out let's grind
I got something to say to stimulate ya mind

The Possibilities of Love

I dream of forehead kisses and unexpected flowers
Having mind blowing sex for hours upon hours
Being well taken care of; no worries for money
Waking up every day to an "I love you honey"

I want a man that loves me more than life
One who takes care of and adores his wife
One who will sacrifice all for his kids
As his head hits the pillow and he closes his lids

Every night the last image he sees is my face
I dream of dancing in a man's warm embrace
A man that from clay God has shaped just for me
I have faith love is possible; in my heart joy can be

ABOUT THE AUTHOR

Amaris Bee is a young and vibrant Atlanta Peach. She is a 15 year veteran of public education and has a doctorate degree. She has attained many accolades from her performance skills and artistic talents. She loves to dance, is a classical pianist, and loves to paint and teach and share with others her God given talent. She began writing this book in her senior year of college. It is a true montage of experiences she has endured throughout her life. This is a collection of the trials and tribulations of her relationships and brief encounters with men. She hopes that you can relate to her stories, learn the lesson, and enjoy. Believe that there is a possibility of finding true love.

The End

www.ingramcontent.com/pod-product-compliance
Lightning Source LLC
Chambersburg PA
CBHW070324100426
42743CB00011B/2553